Good News For All

William MacDonald

Developed as a study course by Emmaus Correspondence School, founded in 1942.

ECS Ministries exists to Glorify God by providing Biblically sound resources and structured study material to teach people from every nation to know Jesus Christ as Savior and to live in a way consistent with God's Word.

Good News for All

William MacDonald

Published by:
Emmaus Worldwide
PO Box 1028
Dubuque, IA 52004-1028
phone: (563) 585-2070
email: info@emmausworldwide.org
website: www.EmmausWorldwide.org

First Edition 2016 (AK '16), 1 Unit
Revised 2017 (AK '17), 1 Unit
Revised 2021 (AK '21), 1 Unit

ISBN 978-1-59387-243-4

Code: GNA

Text Copyright © 2016 William MacDonald
Course Copyright © 2016, 2017, 2021 Emmaus Worldwide

Previously published as The Letter to the Romans, copyright © 1953, 1970, 2002, 2005, 2011 by William MacDonald, published by Emmaus Worldwide.

All rights in this course are reserved. No part of this publication may be reproduced or transmitted in any manner, electronic or mechanical, including photocopy, recording, or any information storage and retrieval system including the Internet without written permission from the publisher. Permission is not needed for brief quotations embodied in critical articles and reviews.

All Scripture quotations, unless otherwise indicated, are taken from the New King James Version. Copyright © 1979, 1980, 1982 by Thomas Nelson, Inc. Used by permission. All rights reserved.

Printed in the United States of America

Course Overview

In this concise study of Paul's letter to the church in Rome, we will learn step by step that the gospel is "the power of God to salvation for everyone who believes." Paul proclaims God's plan to provide deliverance for sinful man from the penalty, power, and eventual presence of sin through Christ's sacrificial death. We learn how to respond to God's grace and mercy in our daily lives, and we gain insights into God's future plan for His earthly people, Israel.

Luther described Romans as "The Purest Gospel." This course serves as an excellent introduction to it.

Lessons You Will Study

Student Instructions

This Emmaus course is designed to help you know God through a better understanding of the Bible and know how it applies to your life. However, this course can never take the place of the Bible itself. The Bible is inexhaustible, and no course could give the full meaning of its truth. If studying this course is the end goal, it will become an obstacle to your growth; if it is used to inspire and equip you for your own personal study of the Bible, then it will achieve its goal. As you study the Bible using this course, prayerfully ask God to reveal His truth to you in a powerful way.

Course Sections

This course has three parts: the *lessons*, the *exams* and the *answer sheet*.

The Lessons

Each lesson is written to help explain truths from the Bible. Read each lesson through at least twice—once to get a general idea of its content, then again, slowly, looking up any Bible references given. You should always have your Bible opened to the verses or passage being studied. It is important that you read the Bible passages referenced, as some questions in the exams may be based on the Bible text.

To look up a Bible verse, keep in mind that passages in the Bible are listed by book, chapter, and verse. For instance, 2 Peter 1:21 refers to the second book of Peter, chapter 1, and verse 21. At the beginning of every Bible, there is a table of contents which lists the names of the books of the Bible and tells the page number on which each book begins. For practice, look up 2 Peter in the table of contents and turn to the page number listed; then find the chapter and verse.

The Exams

At the end of each lesson, there is an exam to assess your knowledge of the course material and the Bible passages. The exams contain multiple choice and/or True/False (T/F) questions. After you have studied a lesson, complete the exam for that lesson by recording your answers on the exam sheet that has been provided. If you have difficulty answering the questions, re-read the lesson or use the Bible as a reference.

Please note, it is best not to answer the questions based on what you *think* or have *always believed*. The questions are designed to find out if you understand the material in the course and the Bible.

What Do You Say?

In addition to the multiple choice section, each exam also contains a *What Do You Say?* question. These questions are designed for your personal reflection and to help you express your ideas and feelings as you process the lesson's content.

The Answer Sheet

Use the answer sheet provided by your group leader or instructor. When you have determined the right answer to a question on an exam, fill in the corresponding letter on the answer sheet. If you do not have someone who could provide an answer sheet, you can download one at www.emmausworldwide.org/answersheets

Submitting the Answer Sheet

When you have answered all the exam questions on the answer sheet, check them carefully. Fill in your contact information and submit your completed answer sheet to your group leader or instructor or the organization from which you received it (several options for submission are shown at next page).

OPTION 1: Send to your group leader or instructor

If you know your group leader or instructor, give them your completed answer sheet or mail it to the address listed here (if blank, go to option 2).

OPTION 2: Send to Emmaus Worldwide's head office

If no address is listed above, or if you do not know if you have a group leader or instructor and are unsure of where to send your answer sheet, choose one of the following:

MAIL the exam sheet to

Emmaus Worldwide
PO Box 1028
Dubuque, IA 52004-1028

OR

EMAIL a scan or photo

of both sides of the answer sheet to this email address:

Exams@EmmausWorldwide.org

Receiving Your Results

You will receive back your graded exam sheet (through the same method it was submitted, either mail or email), including your final grade and a personal response from your group leader or instructor or a representative of Emmaus Worldwide.

LESSON 1

Paul and His Plans

Romans 1:1-17

One of the easiest ways to understand this letter (epistle) is to think of it as a series of questions and answers. As the apostle Paul wrote the letter, he was undoubtedly aware of difficulties that would arise in the minds of some, and of serious objections which would be raised by others. He therefore seems to mention these problems one by one; then he proceeds to answer them in a way that shows this book of the Bible to be truly inspired of God.

We will think of the letter as containing eleven main questions. If the student learns these questions, and the answers Paul supplies, he will at least have a working knowledge of the letter. The questions are as follows:

1. What is the subject of the letter?
2. What is the gospel?
3. Why do people need the gospel?
4. According to the gospel, how can sinners be made acceptable to a holy God?
5. Does the gospel agree with the teaching of the Old Testament Scriptures?
6. What are the benefits of the gospel in a person's life?
7. Does the teaching of the gospel (salvation by faith alone) encourage—or even permit—sinful living?
8. Does the gospel tell Christians to keep the Mosaic law in order to lead a holy life?

9. How, then, is the Christian enabled to live a holy life?
10. Does the gospel, in proclaiming salvation for Gentiles as well as Jews, mean that God has broken His promises to the Jews?
11. How should Christians treat one another?

While studying these lessons, it will be necessary to use a few biblical terms such as *righteousness* and *justification*. However, these words will be explained as clearly as possible when they first appear, as it is important that the student thoroughly understands their meaning.

We proceed now to our study of Romans by considering the questions in order.

"What is the subject of Romans?"

The righteousness of God is revealed in the gospel.

The theme of this letter is the gospel. Paul introduces it almost immediately. After identifying himself as the writer, he tells us that, by a divine summons of Jesus Christ, he has been sent forth to preach the gospel (v. 1). As we shall see, he mentions the gospel three other times in this first chapter—in verses 9, 15 and 16. The readers of the letter are called *saints,* which means "set apart ones" (v. 7).

"What is the gospel?" (vv. 1-17)

First of all, let's answer this question by referring to the dictionary. We learn there that the word itself simply means *good news*. Paul tells us at least six important facts about the gospel in this section:

1. It is the gospel of God (v. 1). This means that God is the author of the good news. It was not made up by man.
2. The gospel was promised by the prophets of the Old Testament Scriptures (v. 2). This remark might have been made especially for the benefit of Jewish people who believed the Old Testament but who resented the gospel as a new and false teaching. They refused to believe that Jesus of Nazareth was the Messiah-Deliverer whom God had promised to send.
3. The gospel is good news concerning God's Son, the Lord Jesus Christ (v. 3). In fact, the gospel is all about Him, this wonderful person who is descended from David as far as His humanity is concerned, but who is demonstrated to be the eternal Son of

God by His resurrection from the dead (v. 4). He is both God and Man.
4. The gospel is God's power to salvation (v. 16). It is the instrument He uses for saving every person who believes on Christ.
5. The gospel is for all people, for Gentiles as well as Jews (v. 16). This is a very important point. The Jews, to whom Paul often preached, hated to hear this. In this letter, Paul has to stress frequently that the good news is for all, and he proves it from the Scriptures, the Old Testament.
6. The gospel is the good news that people are saved by faith alone (v. 17). Here we come to the heart of the gospel message. God saves people on the principle of *believing* and not of *doing*.

The Gospel Demands Righteousness

In verse 17, the word "righteousness" appears for the first time in the letter. We shall therefore pause to consider its meaning. Actually, the word is used in several different ways in the New Testament, but we shall consider only three at this time.

First of all, it is used to describe that characteristic of God by which He always does what is right, just, and proper. When we say that God is righteous, we mean that there is no unfairness, dishonesty, or wrong in Him. Here in verse 17 we learn that the righteousness of God is revealed in the gospel. In other words, the gospel tells how God can save ungodly sinners and still be just in doing so.

The gospel is the good news that people are saved by believing, not doing.

Second, the righteousness of God is used to describe the standard of perfection which God demands of His creatures (Rom. 10:3). Since He Himself is righteous, He requires absolute righteousness from those who would dwell with Him in heaven. As we shall see, man is unable to achieve this righteousness by his own efforts.

Finally, the righteousness of God refers to the perfect standing which God provides for those who believe on His Son, the Lord Jesus Christ. Thus those who are not in themselves righteous are treated as if they *were* righteous because God sees them in all the perfection of Christ (2 Cor. 5:21).

In the opening seventeen verses of his letter, Paul has introduced his subject and stated very briefly some of the main points which he will explain in greater detail as he proceeds.

CHAPTER 1 EXAM

Use the exam sheet that has been provided to complete your exam.

1. **This letter can be understood as**
   A. a serious lecture.
   B. a series of questions and answers.
   C. a reply to a previous letter from the Roman church.

2. **In view of Paul's emphasis in Romans, what would be the best title for the letter?**
   A. I, Paul
   B. Beware of the Cult
   C. The Gospel

3. **Paul addresses the readers of this letter as**
   A. Gentiles.
   B. saints.
   C. Romans.

4. **_______ is the author (originator) of the gospel.**
   A. God
   B. Paul
   C. Man

5. **The gospel**
   A. was promised by the prophets of the Old Testament.
   B. was thought up by God when Jesus was crucified.
   C. was developed gradually by the church.

6. **The word "gospel" means**
   A. exciting news.
   B. bad news.
   C. good news.

7. Jesus was demonstrated to be the eternal Son of God by His
   A. crucifixion.
   B. resurrection.
   C. life.

8. God saves people on the principle of
   A. doing good works and being baptized.
   B. believing on Jesus and doing good works.
   C. believing in the Lord Jesus Christ.

9. In verse 17 we learn that the righteousness of God is revealed
   A. through preaching.
   B. through our intuition.
   C. in the gospel.

10. Among other things, "the righteousness of God" refers to
   A. the perfect standing God provides to those who believe in His Son.
   B. the judgment God will bring on His enemies.
   C. God's ability to see everything in creation.

What Do You Say?

How can you be sure that you are righteous enough to go to heaven? Explain your answer.

____

____

____

____

LESSON 2

The Sin Question

Romans 1:18–3:20

In the previous lesson we discussed the question, "What is the gospel?" We discovered that it originates with God; it was promised in the Old Testament; it is centered in the Lord Jesus; and it is a powerful force for bringing all who believe it into a right standing with God. In this lesson we are going to ask another question:

"Why do people need the gospel?"

Apart from the gospel, mankind is condemned and in imminent danger of hell.

The answer, in brief, is that all human beings are ungodly sinners and are therefore exposed to the awful wrath of God. We are told in verse 18 that "the wrath of God is revealed from heaven against all ungodliness and unrighteousness of men, who suppress the truth in unrighteousness." Apart from the gospel, mankind, without any exceptions, is condemned and in imminent danger of hell. We will use the word "lost" to describe man's condition.

1. The Heathen (1:18-32)

Now, one of man's favorite arguments, when told that he is lost, is this: What about the heathen who have never heard the gospel of Christ? This age-old question is answered in verses 19-32.

Every person may know that there is a God by the works of creation (vv. 19-20). God's eternal power and deity are demonstrated by the sun, the moon, the stars, the human body, animal and vegetable life, and in many other ways. He expects man to recognize Him as Maker, to glorify Him as God, and to be thankful for His creation, preservation, and every other blessing.

The trouble is, however, that man has rejected the witness of creation to God (vv. 21-22). For this reason, he is without excuse. Instead of worshiping the only true God, he made idols resembling human beings, birds, animals, and snakes. These became his gods (v. 23).

Of course, such dead idols cannot inspire people to live holy lives. Rather, they worshiped these false gods so they could indulge in all kinds of sin without fear of punishment. They refused the true God and substituted carved images so they could live as they pleased. Accordingly, "God also gave them up to uncleanness" (v. 24); man went deeper and deeper into moral darkness and sexual immorality to the point that they "exchanged the natural use for what is against nature" (v. 26.) From then on, man's life became filled with the terrible sins of verses 29-31, and he took added pleasure in encouraging others to do likewise.

2. The Jews (2:1–3:8)

Having demonstrated that the heathen, or Gentile, is lost, Paul now takes up the case of the Jews. Surely, this privileged people to whom God gave *the Law*—moral laws and ceremonial rites—is not under condemnation! But yes, the Jew is lost in sin as well.

While criticizing their Gentile neighbors, the Jews were committing the same sins themselves (2:1). Because God did not punish them immediately, they thought they were getting away with it (v. 3). Actually, God was simply giving them time to repent (v. 4), but they kept on sinning, thus increasing their guilt at the day of judgment (v. 5).

God's judgment will surely come, however. Verses 2-16 give the principles on which God's judgment is based. If a man could show that by persevering in well-doing he sought for glory and honor and immortality, he would be rewarded eternal life (vv. 7-10). However, this passage does not teach that any can ever be saved in this way. On the contrary, chapter 3:19-20 conclusively prove that no one will ever be saved by good works.

God's judgment would be strictly impartial, whether of the Jews or Gentiles (v. 11). Those to whom the Law was given would be judged according to the Law (v. 12). The Gentiles, to whom no law was given, would be judged by the voice of their own conscience, which told them what was right and wrong (vv. 14-15).

The Jews were proud of their many privileges as God's earthly people (vv. 17-20), but they did not practice what they preached (vv. 21-23), and so brought reproach on the name of God (v. 24). They needed to realize that religious rites, such as circumcision, are worthless unless a person's life agrees with his profession (vv. 25-29). Circumcision was a ceremony instituted by God in Genesis 17 as a sign of His covenant with Abraham. It was to be practiced on all male members of the family. Because it required a cutting away of flesh, it symbolized God's standard for His people to be a holy people, separated from the world. Israelites commonly referred to Gentiles as "the uncircumcised."

The Gentiles, to whom no law was given, would be judged by the voice of their own conscience.

Does the fact that the Jew is lost mean that there was no advantage to being a Jew (3:1)? No, it does not mean that. There were many advantages, one being that the writing of the Holy Scriptures, the Word of God, was committed to this nation (v. 2). And God will still keep His promises to Israel, despite that nation's unfaithfulness, but He will not overlook their sin (vv. 3-8).

3. The Inevitable Conclusion (3:9-20)

What is the conclusion then? Simply this, that all people, both Jew and Gentile, are sinners. The Old Testament teaches clearly that sin has affected the whole human race (vv. 10-12). It also teaches that sin has affected every part of man—his throat, tongue, lips, mouth, feet, and eyes (vv. 13-18). The Law condemned the Jews who were under it, and, in so doing, condemns everyone. Verse 19 declares that, in God's sight, the Jews are really a sample of the whole human race. God tested the sample under the Law and found it evil. He therefore pronounced the whole race sinful on the basis of the sample. The Law has exposed the guilt of all mankind, so it is obvious that no one can be justified by keeping its commandments.

CHAPTER 2 EXAM

Use the exam sheet that has been provided to complete your exam

1. **Because of the witness of creation, God expects man to**
   A. recognize Him and glorify Him as God.
   B. know about His plan of salvation.
   C. take good care of the environment.

2. **Those who have never heard the gospel of salvation through Christ**
   A. are lost, since they do not know better.
   B. are lost because God does not love them.
   C. are lost by rejecting the witness of God in creation.

3. **The basic reason why men resort to idolatry is that**
   A. idols are a true representation of God.
   B. it frees men from moral restraint.
   C. all religions evolve from idolatry.

4. **Chapter 3:19-20 proves that**
   A. a man with good intentions toward God will be saved.
   B. only Jews can be saved.
   C. no one will ever be saved by good works.

5. **According to Romans 2:2-16, God's judgment is**
   A. partial to the Jews.
   B. impartial to Jews and Gentiles.
   C. partial to those who live good lives.

6. **According to Romans 2, how would God judge the Gentiles?**
   A. based on the law
   B. based on their own consciences
   C. they would not be judged

7. **The Jews were given the law by God. As a result, they**
   A. sincerely kept God's law.
   B. had an exclusive claim on God.
   C. were inflated with religious pride.

8. **____________ was a ceremony instituted by God as a sign of His covenant with Abraham.**
   A. Baptism
   B. Circumcision
   C. Communion

9. **Which of the following is an advantage of being a Jew?**
   A. They were given many gods to choose from.
   B. They were chosen to fulfill God's Law perfectly.
   C. They were entrusted with writing the Holy Scriptures.

10. **The Law**
    A. exposed the guilt of all mankind.
    B. explains the righteousness of the Jews.
    C. provides the only way to be saved.

What Do You Say?

What have you learned about your own heart in this lesson?

____

____

____

____

LESSON 3

Salvation

Romans 3:21-31

Up to this point in our studies, we have seen that all human beings are sinners and therefore subject to the wrath of God. A holy God must see that sins are punished, and the punishment He has decreed for sin is death. The great question then is this:

"How can sinners become acceptable to a holy God?"

In the verses now before us, Paul sets forth the doctrine of *justification* as the answer. This is a very important section, containing tremendous truths in condensed form. Before proceeding, however, we must examine the meaning of justification as set forth in the New Testament.

1. What Justification Is

Justification is the act by which God counts a sinner as absolutely fit for heaven the moment he or she believes on the Lord Jesus Christ.

It does not mean that the believer becomes sinless or righteous in himself. Rather, God covers him, as it were, with a robe of righteousness. God now sees him as being in Christ and he is accepted—not because of who he is, but because of Christ's person and work.

Some have defined "justified" this way: just-as-if-I'd never sinned. Others have expressed it like this: just-as-if-I'd died. These meanings are all right as far as they go. However, they simply state that the penalty of sin has been paid by Christ. Justification goes beyond this, teaching that the believing sinner now has a *perfect standing* before God in Christ.

> "Near, so very near to God,
> I could not nearer be,
> For in the person of His Son
> I am as near as He."

As A. T. Pierson puts it, "God, in justifying sinners, actually calls them righteous when they are not—does not impute sin where sin actually exists—and does impute righteousness where it does not exist." (To *impute* means "to charge, or credit, to one's account." The New Testament speaks of Adam's sin being imputed to every man, and of God's righteousness being imputed to the account of every believer in Christ).

But God does not compromise with sin or tolerate evil in the Christian. He first *reckons* men holy, and then proceeds to *make* them holy. This process, known as *sanctification*, will be completed when the believer is taken home to heaven.

2. How Justification Works

Now let us note carefully how Paul sets forth this thrilling truth. First, we learn in verse 21 that the righteousness of God has been revealed. This means that God has now shown *how* He imputes righteousness to sinners, and is still righteous in doing so. It is "apart from the law." People are not justified by keeping the Ten Commandments, or by human effort of any kind. It was "witnessed by the Law and the Prophets," that is, the Old Testament Scriptures agree with this teaching. It is "through faith in Jesus Christ" (v. 22). This is the means by which sinners are justified. It is "to all and on all who believe" (v. 22). There is no distinction between Jew and Gentile—all have sinned, and therefore all need the righteousness of God. It is offered to all, and imputed to all who believe (vv. 22-23). People are justified "freely by His grace" (v. 24). This not only means that they do not have to pay for salvation, but also that they do not deserve it. The only reason God bothers with man at all is because He is by nature a loving, merciful, gracious God.

The believing sinner now has a perfect standing before God in Christ.

Justification is "through the redemption that is in Christ Jesus." This "redemption," a term that was used to describe the purchasing of a slave from the slave market, is the basis on which God can save man. He could not overlook sin or excuse it. The Law demanded the death of the sinner. God must see that the demands of the Law were met. So He sent His sinless Son to die as a substitute for ungodly men and women, boys and girls. Christ paid the penalty of the broken Law for all who receive Him by faith. Christ has thus become a "propitiation" (v. 25). This means that, by the shedding of His precious blood, all God's righteous demands have been met, propitiated, satisfied. God is *satisfied* with the work of His Son. Therefore, He can now show mercy to those who receive the Savior.

The gospel further explains how God forgave the sins of the people in Old Testament times (v. 25). "The sins that were previously committed" refers to sins committed before Jesus died on Calvary. These were forgiven on the basis of the work of Christ which was still future at that time. Old Testament believers looked forward to Calvary by faith, while today we look back to it. Thus it is clearly shown how God can justify all who believe in Jesus and still be just in doing so (v. 26). His righteousness demanded the death of the sinner, but His love desired the salvation of the lost. By sending His Son to die for us, He solved the problem in a satisfactory manner.

There is no merit attached to believing God. It is the reasonable thing to do.

This plan of salvation eliminates all human boasting (v. 27). If people could be saved by doing something, then they might boast. But there is no merit attached to believing God. It is the *reasonable* thing to do.

The conclusion, then, is that man is justified by faith alone, and not by obeying the Law (v. 28). This justification is for the Gentiles as well as the Jews (vv. 29-30). The gospel does not do away with the Law (v. 31). The law of God demanded either perfect obedience or the death of the one who broke it. Since everyone has broken God's perfect law in some way, all are guilty of death. But, as we have seen, Christ died to meet the full requirements of the Law for the sinner. When we preach salvation by faith, we uphold the Law by insisting that its utmost demands have been fully met.

The glorious truth of justification has been beautifully expressed in a poem by Albert Midlane, entitled "The Perfect Righteousness of God."

> The perfect righteousness of God
> Is witnessed in the Savior's blood;
> 'Tis in the cross of Christ we trace
> His righteousness, yet wondrous grace.

God could not pass the sinner by,
The law demands that he must die;
But in the cross of Christ we see
How God can save, yet righteous be.
The sin alights on Jesus' head,
'Tis in His blood sin's debt is paid;
Stern Justice can demand no more,
And Mercy can dispense her store.
The sinner who believes is free,
Can say, "The Savior died for me;"
Can point to the atoning blood,
And say, "This made my peace with God."

CHAPTER 3 EXAM

Use the exam sheet that has been provided to complete your exam

1. **The punishment that God has decreed for sin is**
   A. public service.
   B. jail time.
   C. death.

2. **According to the New Testament doctrine of justification,**
   A. God counts a sinner fit for heaven the moment he believes.
   B. a person becomes righteous in himself when he believes.
   C. a believer can love as he wants.

3. **Sanctification is the process whereby God**
   A. makes men holy and then reckons them holy.
   B. reckons men holy and then makes them holy.
   C. makes men so holy that they become sinless.

4. **Which person is justified in the sight of God?**
   A. The one who keeps God's law as an ethical rule
   B. The one who believes in Christ as his personal Savior
   C. The one who lives a religious life

5. **"Being justified freely by His grace" means**
   A. God's salvation is conditional.
   B. man can save himself.
   C. salvation is free and undeserved.

6. **The righteous demands of the Old Testament law**
   A. are ignored in the gospel.
   B. make salvation dependent on faith and works.
   C. were fully met by the death of Jesus Christ.

7. Propitiation means

A. God's anger against sin has been reduced.
B. God's righteous demands have been met at Calvary.
C. God will pardon sinners who live a good life.

8. Which of the following is true?

A. Before Christ's death men were saved by works.
B. Faith in Christ is always the basis for salvation.
C. Animal sacrifices were sufficient for salvation.

9. According to Romans 3:27-28, if men could be saved by doing something,

A. God would share His glory with them.
B. there'd be more people going to heaven.
C. then they might boast.

10. The gospel

A. upholds the Law.
B. replaces the Law.
C. ignores the Law.

What Do You Say?

Are you justified in God's sight? Explain your answer.

LESSON 4

Justified by Faith

Romans 4:1-25

In our last lesson we learned what it means to be justified. This raises another question:

"Does the gospel agree with the Old Testament?"

Paul has already stated twice that it does, but he is now going to prove it. In doing so, he uses the examples of two men—Abraham, who lived centuries before the Law was given, and David, who lived many years after it was given.

1. The Example of Abraham (vv. 1-5)

How was Abraham justified? If it were by works, then he could boast before God. But this is impossible. No creature can ever boast before the Creator (v. 2). The Old Testament clearly tells how Abraham was saved (Gen. 15:6): he was reckoned (considered) righteous by believing God (v. 3). Thus God justifies the ungodly not by works, but by grace through faith (vv. 4-5). *Grace* is the basis on which God gives salvation. *Faith* is the means by which man receives it.

God justifies the ungodly not by works, but by grace through faith.

2. *The Example of David (vv. 6-8)*

Well then, does David's experience agree with this? Yes, David speaks of the blessedness of the one whom God pronounces righteous not by law-keeping, but simply by being dealt with in grace. He said, for instance, "Blessed are those whose lawless deeds are forgiven, and whose sins are covered." This refers to a pardoned sinner, not an upright law-keeper (v. 7). He said also, "Blessed is the man to whom the Lord shall not impute sin." Here, again, there is no mention of man's efforts. It is all of God's grace (v. 8).

3. *The Question of Circumcision (vv. 9-12)*

But doesn't the Old Testament teach that circumcision was necessary for salvation? The answer is no. Abraham was justified before he was circumcised; he received circumcision later as an outward sign of the righteousness which he had obtained by putting his faith in God. Thus he became the father of all true believers.

All the Law can do is condemn those who fail to keep it.

4. *The Question of the Law (vv. 13-16)*

But isn't law-keeping connected in some way with justification? Not at all. Justification is by grace, and not by law.

When God made His promise to Abraham that he would be heir of the world (through Christ), it was not on the basis of keeping a law. In other words, there were no conditions attached. It was not dependent on any works on Abraham's part. It was simply a promise from God that He would do it (v. 13).

Indeed, if the promise depended on keeping any kind of law, then faith would be unnecessary; the promise would be worthless because no one could meet the terms (v. 14).

All the Law, that God gave, can do is condemn those who fail to keep it (v. 15). Thus God has decreed that salvation should be by grace through faith (v. 16). This is the only way the promise of eternal life might be *sure.* If good works were necessary, we could never be sure we had done enough, or done the right kind works. Also, this is the only way the promise of eternal life might be sure to *all.* If man was required to *do* something to be saved, there would always be some people who could not meet the conditions.

Belief on Christ is the only thing of which every person is capable without, at the same time, achieving any personal merit.

5. More about Abraham (vv. 17-25)

Abraham's case proves conclusively that justification is by faith (vv. 17-22). God promised Abraham that he would be the father of many nations. He told him that he would have descendants as numerous as the stars (vv. 17-18). Humanly speaking, this was impossible. Abraham himself was about one hundred years old, and his wife was too old to bear children. Up until this point in time, they did not have any family. Yet God had made the promise, and so Abraham dared to believe, knowing that God could perform the impossible.

God has promised eternal life to those who receive Christ by faith.

> "Faith, mighty faith, the promise sees,
> And looks to God alone,
> Laughs at impossibilities,
> And cries, 'It shall be done.'"

"Therefore 'it was accounted to him for righteousness'" (v. 22).

Abraham's history was written as a lesson to us (vv. 23-25). He was not the only example of where righteousness is imputed to a man by faith. God will do the same for us if our faith is in Him—the One who raised the Lord Jesus from the dead. He has promised eternal life to those who receive Christ by faith. Just as Christ was delivered to die on the cross because of our sins, so God raised Him from the dead in order that we might be justified through Him. Christ's resurrection is a proof that God is satisfied with His work on Calvary.

CHAPTER 4 EXAM

Use the exam sheet that has been provided to complete your exam

1. **The examples of which two Old Testament saints show that the gospel agrees with the Old Testament?**
   A. David who lived before the giving of the law, and Abraham, after
   B. Abraham who lived before the giving of the law, and David, after
   C. Abraham and David, who both lived after the law was given

2. **How was Abraham justified before God? By**
   A. works, which gave him grounds for boasting
   B. works, even though he could not boast
   C. faith, since his faith was counted as righteousness

3. **Which of the following is justified in God's sight?**
   A. One who makes a pilgrimage to religious shrines
   B. One who serves humanity
   C. One who believes in Jesus Christ

4. **What was the basis of David's forgiveness?**
   A. The grace of God alone
   B. The enormous sacrifice he offered
   C. His penance in sackcloth and ashes

5. **What did Abraham and David have in common?**
   A. Both lived after the law was given.
   B. Both kept the law perfectly.
   C Because of their faith, God did not count their sins against them.

6. **How does Paul show that there is no merit in rites? By**
   A. stating that Jews need not be circumcised.
   B. showing that Abraham was justified before circumcision.
   C. declaring that baptism had replaced circumcision.

7. **Abraham's righteousness**
   A. was guaranteed by an unconditional promise.
   B. was dependent on his being circumcised.
   C. was dependent on his keeping the law after he believed.

8. **All that the Law can do is**
   A. justify those who obey it.
   B. help make all people perfect.
   C. condemn those who fail to keep it.

9. **Abraham's history was written**
   A. as a lesson to us of faith.
   B. to show us how only Israelites will be saved.
   C. to show us that circumcision is necessary.

10. **The resurrection of Christ is**
   A. proof that Christ did not die on the cross.
   B. proof that God is satisfied with Christ's work on Calvary.
   C. proof that the Christ's death does not matter.

What Do You Say?

In what sense is Abraham "the father of us all"?

LESSON 5

Adam and Christ

Romans 5:1-21

Having explained the doctrine of justification by faith, Paul now turns his attention to the effects of this in the believer's life. He is actually answering the very practical question, "Does it really work?"

"What are the practical benefits of the gospel?"

In the verses that follow, he piles proof upon proof that the blessings of justification are wonderfully real. Note that all these blessings flow to the believer through the Lord Jesus Christ. He is the Mediator between God and man, and all God's gifts are received through Him.

1. The Fruits of Justification (vv. 1-11)

Paul sets forth six fruits of justification:

1. We have peace with God through our Lord Jesus Christ (v. 1). Formerly, we were at enmity with God. We fought against Him. We did not want Him to rule over us. But now the warfare has ended. We have surrendered unconditionally. A state of peace exists.
2. We have access by faith into this grace in which we stand (v. 2). The word "grace" conveys the wonderful place of blessing and favor with God into which we have been brought by the Savior.

3. We rejoice in hope of the glory of God. It is a joy to look forward to the time when God's glory will be seen by a wondering universe. All Christians share this hope.
4. We glory in tribulation (v. 3). We could not rejoice in trials when we were unsaved, but now we realize that only in this way can God produce certain godly traits in our lives, such as patience, character, and hope.
5. We have the unshakable confidence that our hope will never be disappointed (v. 5). Christ will see us safely home to heaven. How can we be so sure? Because the Holy Spirit fills our hearts with the following proofs of God's eternal love to us. It was when we were without strength and ungodly that Christ died for us (v. 6). Will He do less for us now that we belong to Him? Christ died for us, not when we were decent or even good, but when we were sinners. Now that we are justified, will He not save us from judgment (vv. 7-9)? When we were enemies we were reconciled to God. To reconcile means to remove causes of enmity or unfriendliness, or to settle differences and to bring together in harmony. Surely now that we are His friends, He will preserve us (v. 10). We were reconciled to God by the death of His Son. Death speaks of weakness. If Christ's seeming weakness and defeat were sufficiently powerful to reconcile us to God, how much more will the power of His endless life ensure our complete and final salvation (v. 10)!

We have the unshakable confidence that our hope will never be disappointed.

6. We rejoice in God (v. 11). This is quite a change. Before our conversion, we had no pleasure in God at all. In fact, it was only when we could forget Him that we were happy. However, now that we have been reconciled to God through Christ, we enjoy Him as the One who is nearest and dearest to us.

Thus the apostle concludes his catalog of the results of the Savior's work for the believer. In the verses to follow, he is going to gather up the threads of the argument so far in the letter.

2. The Summing Up (vv. 12-21)

Two main subjects have occupied our attention up to this point, namely, *condemnation* and *justification*. Adam brought the former on the human race, and the Lord Jesus provided the latter. Now notice how Paul compares and contrasts the two.

Sin and death entered the world through Adam (v. 12). In reality, Adam acted as a representative of all mankind. We can illustrate it this way: When the ruler of a nation signs an official document, he signs it for all the people in the nation; he is acting for them. Thus when Adam sinned, the results of his act affected the entire race. When he sinned, all sinned, and death came upon all (v. 12).

This is proved in an interesting way. During the period from Adam to Moses, people did not have a law from God. They did not disobey any *written* commandments of God. Yet people died during this time because sin and death had entered the world through Adam, and enslaved all people.

By the work of the Lord Jesus, the tyranny of sin and death has been ended.

Adam is a figure, or type, of Christ (v. 14b). Just as Adam acted as a representative for his race, so the Lord Jesus came to act in behalf of a new "race." But notice some striking contrasts in the next verses.

It is true that because of the transgression of one man, many have died. But think how much greater God's grace is than man's sin—and not only God's grace, but the gift which flows out to many through Christ (v. 15).

The effect of one man's sin was that all human beings were sentenced to condemnation. How much greater is the effect of God's gift! In Christ there is not only freedom from condemnation, but a perfect standing before God. And this is true in spite of not just one sin, but many sins (v. 16).

By the one sin of one man, death reigned as a cruel tyrant. But by the gracious gift of Christ, men themselves reign like kings, enjoying the life which the Savior gives them (v. 17). Thus, just as by the sin of one man all people were condemned, so by Christ's "one righteous act"—His substitutionary death at the cross—justification is provided for all (v. 18).

And as many were made sinners by Adam's disobedience, so by Christ's obedience in death, the many who trust Him will be declared righteous (v. 19).

God gave the Law so the awfulness of sin might be seen in its true light. But God's grace at Calvary was seen to be greater than all man's sin.

By the work of the Lord Jesus, the tyranny of sin and death has been ended, and those who trust Him are better off than if Adam had never sinned (vv. 20-21). As long as Adam remained innocent, he could look forward to a long life on earth. But he had no promise of becoming a child of God, an heir of God, and a joint-heir with the Son of God. He did not have the prospect of a home in heaven, or of being intimately united with Jesus Christ and like Him forever.

Through the work of Christ, the believer has all these blessings, and many more as well. Thus it will be seen that

> "In Christ the sons of Adam boast
> More blessings than their father lost."

Perhaps this is a partial answer to the familiar question as to why God allowed sin to enter into the world: Not only has man received more blessings through the sacrificial work of Christ than if there never had been any sins to be put away, but God has gained more glory.

CHAPTER 5 EXAM

Use the exam sheet that has been provided to complete your exam

1. **The blessings inherent in the gospel come to the believer**
   A. only through Christ.
   B. only as a result of prayer and fasting.
   C. only when he lives a sinless life.

2. **The first fruit of justification mentioned in Romans 5 is**
   A. new love for the brethren.
   B. peace with God.
   C. freedom from any temptation to sin.

3. **"This grace in which we stand" is**
   A. liberty from sin and liberty to sin.
   B. assurance of material prosperity.
   C. a wonderful place of favor with God.

4. **Which of the following is true?**
   A. The believer will have no tribulations.
   B. God will use the trials of a Christian for his good.
   C. Trials are always a judgment from God.

5. **One reason a believer can be absolutely sure of heaven is**
   A. because he regular attends church.
   B. that he has been baptized.
   C. that Christ is alive and will keep him.

6. **The two truths Paul emphasized in his summary are**
   A. justification and sanctification.
   B. condemnation and justification.
   C. faith and works.

7. **The consequences of being "in Adam" are that**
   A. all have human rights.
   B. all are born sinners and subject to death.
   C. everyone will enjoy eternity in heaven.

8. **Just as Adam was the representative for all people born after he sinned, so Jesus Christ is the representative for**
   A. all who read the Bible.
   B. all who never sin.
   C. all who trust Him to save them.

9. **Which of the following is greater?**
   A. Man's sin
   B. God's grace
   C. Man's need

10. **One thing that the believer enjoys above anything Adam anticipated is**
    A. that he is a child and heir of God.
    B. that he does not have to toil on the land.
    C. that he does not battle with Satan.

What Do You Say?

Which one of the six results of justification mentioned in chapter 5 is the most meaningful to you, and why?

LESSON 6

On to Victory

Romans 6:1-23

We have seen that we can be justified with God by faith alone and not by works. This truth raises a question in the minds of some:

"Does the gospel permit sinful living?"

When the gospel of grace is preached, people often make the following objection: "If all you have to do to be saved is believe on Christ, then you can go out and live as you please." In this chapter we learn why this is impossible.

1. Knowing (vv. 1-10)

The first great fact we meet is that Christians have "died to sin" (v. 2). What does this mean? Simply this: our old nature has been crucified—condemned to death—with Christ. God was not interested in patching up or improving our evil, corrupt nature. His only remedy for it was death. When the Savior died, He died as our *representative.* In God's estimation, when He died, we died. All that we were by nature was nailed to Calvary's cross. Likewise, when Christ was buried, we were buried. That removed us out of God's sight forever as sinful creatures. Our old "I" has been put in its proper place—the grave.

In God's estimation, when Christ died, we died. All that we were by nature was nailed to the cross.

This is all pictured by baptism (vv. 3-7). When we go beneath the water, we witness that we, as children of Adam, deserved nothing but death. We agree with God that our old self, or "old man," was unfit to live. We confess that we died with Christ and were buried with Him. Since Christ died to settle the whole question of sin once and for all, we admit that we no longer have any right to practice sin. We are dead to sin, not in the sense that we are sinless, but in the sense that God sees us as those who have died, and therefore sin has no claim upon us.

But Christ rose from the dead, and since we are in Christ, God sees *us* as having risen also (vv. 8-10). However, we do not rise to live the same old kind of a life. We rise as new creatures with the object that Christ may from now on live His life in us.

Now, these are divine facts. Whether you *feel* them to be true or not, God says that every justified person is dead to sin, buried with Christ, risen with Him, and given a new life—His life. He wants you to *know* that this is true of you as far as your position before Him is concerned. He wants you to accept it by faith.

2. Reckoning (vv. 11-12)

The next step is to "Reckon yourself to be dead indeed to sin, but alive to God" (vv. 11-12). It is already so as to your standing; now let it be so as to your practice. Behave as one who is dead to sin, self, and the world, and alive to God. Do not let sin reign over you. Remember that you have died to its power and claims over you.

3. Yielding (v. 13)

Finally, the Christian is to yield himself to God (v. 13). Let God control you. Turn over the members of your body—your lips, your mind, your hands, etc.—to Him daily, yes, continually. Then, instead of living your own life and doing the things you want to do, you will allow Him to live His life in you.

4. Under Grace, Not Law (vv. 14-23)

Sin does not have dominion over the believer because he is not under law but under grace (v. 14). This is an important point.

When a man is under law, sin has dominion over him. The Law tells him what to do but does not give him the power to do it. Moreover, when you tell a sinful person not to do a certain thing, he immediately wants to do it all the more.

The Christian is under grace. Whereas law says, "Live a holy life and you will be a Christian," grace says, "You are a Christian by God's free gift; now live a holy life out of love for Him." People will do out of love what they would never do by compulsion or from fear of punishment.

The fact that the Christian is not under law does not mean he will want to live in sin. He has been given a new nature which hates sin. He is indwelt by the Holy Spirit of God who encourage and enables him to live a holy life. He remembers what his sins cost the Savior. He knows that he is the servant of whomever he obeys. He used to obey sin, but now he is ashamed of that kind of a life (vv. 16-21).

People will do out of love what they would never do by compulsion or from fear of punishment.

The great desire of the child of God, therefore, is to yield himself as a servant of God so that the life of Christ might be reproduced in him (vv. 22-23).

CHAPTER 6 EXAM

Use the exam sheet that has been provided to complete your exam

1. **The believer in the Lord Jesus is**
   A. dead in sin.
   B. dead to sin.
   C. very much alive to sin.

2. **According to Romans 6 the believer's "old man" has been**
   A. eradicated altogether.
   B. crucified with Christ.
   C. cleansed by God.

3. **In Romans 6, what picture is used to describe what happened to our old nature?**
   A. Marriage
   B. Birth
   C. Baptism

4. **The aspect of Christ's resurrection emphasized in Romans 6 is**
   A. the historical fact of it.
   B. the believer's share in it spiritually here and now.
   C. the guarantee of a bodily resurrection.

5. **What practical steps sum up victorious living?**
   A. Love, joy, and peace
   B. Faith, hope, and love
   C. Know, reckon, and yield

6. **What is to be the believer's attitude toward his body?**
   A. He is to indulge its desires.
   B. He is to yield its members to God.
   C. He is to punish it because of sin.

7. **Sin no longer has the right to rule the believer because**
   A. he or she is indwelt by the Holy Spirit.
   B. he or she is under grace and not law.
   C. he or she is dead to temptation.

8. **What should motivate us to holy living?**
   A. Discipline – "I have to"
   B. Duty – "I ought to"
   C. Devotion – "I want to"

9. **A true Christian chooses not to live a sinful life because**
   A. he has a new nature which hates sin.
   B. the Holy Spirit enables him to live righteously.
   C. both A and B are correct.

10. **The Christian is to be**
   A. the slave of his circumstances.
   B. the bondslave of the Lord Jesus.
   C. a slave to good works.

What Do You Say?

Give one example of how you have applied the teaching of Romans 6 to your life.

____

____

____

____

LESSON 7

Bondage!

Romans 7:1-25

Paul has previously shown very clearly that man is not saved by keeping the Law. But now another question arises:

"Must we keep the Law once we are saved?"

After a person is saved, is he not obliged to keep the Mosaic law (in essence, the Ten Commandments) as a rule of life?

In the previous chapter, we learned that the Christian is not under law but under grace. The reason for this will now be made plain. In addition, the apostle will demonstrate from his own experience the impossibility of a believer's achieving holiness by his own efforts.

The child of God has become dead to the law of God because he has now become intimately united with the body of Christ.

1. Free from the Law (vv. 1-6)

The principle Paul expounds here is that law has no authority over a person after he dies. This is illustrated by the law of marriage. This law binds man and wife together only as long as they are both alive. However, when one of them dies, the authority of the law is ended, and the living partner is free to marry again (vv. 1-3).

The child of God has become dead to the law of God because he has now become intimately united with the body of Christ (v. 4). The Lord

Jesus died to the Law in the sense that He paid the penalty it demanded for transgressions against it. Since the believer has been crucified with Christ, he too has died to the Law. And since all its demands have been met in the death of the Savior, the Law has nothing more to say to the Christian.

This freedom from the Law enables the believer to be united to Christ, who is raised from the dead (v. 4). The Lord Jesus—not the Law—becomes the believer's rule of life. Marriage implies union. Union with Christ means sharing His life. It is far better to allow the life of Christ to be manifested in our mortal bodies than to seek to become holy by our own feeble efforts.

Freedom from the Law enables us to bring forth fruit for God (v. 4). When the Law forbids a certain thing, the human heart desires to do it all the more. Since the penalty for breaking God's perfect standards set forth in the Law is death, and since none of us has the power to keep it, the only "fruit" we can bring forth under it is death (v. 5). Now that we, as Christians, are delivered from the Law, we can serve the Lord with willing hearts, and not out of compulsion or fear (v. 6).

2. The Function of the Law (vv. 7-14)

Does this mean that the Law itself is sinful? The apostle emphasizes that it is not. Its very holiness reveals the greatness of man's sin. Paul would not have known, for instance, that evil thoughts, as well as wicked acts, are sinful except for the law that said, "You shall not covet" (v. 7). But our sinful, corrupt nature uses the Law to stir up all manner of evil desires within us, so that we long to do that which is forbidden. Thus, apart from the Law, sin might be thought of as a sleeping thing. But when the Law comes, sin wakens and becomes very active (vv. 8-11). The conclusion, then, is that the Law is holy, just, and good, showing sin in all its wickedness. But the human heart is depraved and wants to do what it is told not to do (vv. 12-14).

The Lord Jesus —not the Law— becomes the believer's rule of life.

3. Trying Too Hard (vv. 15-25)

Attempts to lead a holy life by one's own efforts lead to disappointment and despair. Paul cites his own experience in this connection (vv. 15-24).

He knew what he ought to do, but he could not do it. The things that he hated, those were the things he did. He acknowledged that the Law was good, but his old nature was hopelessly unable to obey it. The more he tried to do what was right, the more he seemed to fail. Finally, he came to the end of himself and was forced to confess defeat: "O wretched man that I am! Who will deliver me from this body of death?" (v. 24).

The secret of holiness is not found in ourselves, but in the Lord Jesus Christ.

It was then, and not until then, that Paul realized that the secret of holiness was not to be found in himself, but in the Lord Jesus Christ. "I thank God—through Jesus Christ our Lord" was his shout of triumph. It was only as Paul allowed the Lord to live His life in and through him that Paul experienced any measure of deliverance from indwelling sin (v. 25).

CHAPTER 7 EXAM

Use the exam sheet that has been provided to complete your exam

1. **In Romans 7, what illustrates the believer's relationship to the law?**
   A. Marriage and divorce
   B. Marriage and death
   C. Death and burial

2. **The Lord Jesus died to the Law in the sense that**
   A. He paid the penalty it demanded.
   B. He didn't need to obey it.
   C. He taught that it was worthless.

3. **The demands of the law for the believer**
   A. are met in the death of Christ.
   B. are of no consequence, since the law was given to Israel.
   C. must be met by the believer himself.

4. **What best expresses the believer's relationship to the law?**
   A. He must keep the law to be saved.
   B. He must keep the law to remain saved.
   C. He is dead to the law and achieves holiness apart from it.

5. **The believer's union with Christ is**
   A. a mystical relationship with no practical application.
   B. sharing His life.
   C. is a legal matter.

6. **Which of the commandments made Paul conscious of sin?**
   A. You shall have no other gods before Me.
   B. Honor your father and mother.
   C. You shall not covet (lust).

7. The law

A. gives sin an opportunity to act.
B. produces true holiness of life.
C. produces fruit for God in the believer's life.

8. In Romans 7:7-24, Paul is mostly occupied with

A. the Holy Spirit.
B. the Lord Jesus Christ.
C. himself.

9. Paul finally found the deliverance for which he longed

A. in fasting and prayer.
B. in the law itself.
C. in the Lord Jesus Christ.

10. What counsel would you give to a Christian who has a bad temper?

A. It is a bad habit, and victory is impossible.
B. There are worse sins.
C. It is a serious sin, but you can receive victory through Christ.

What Do You Say?

Are you trusting and obeying Christ in your daily life? Explain.

LESSON 8

Freedom!

Romans 8:1-39

We have already learned that it is not by one's own strength that sin's passions are restrained. In this chapter, we are taught that we gain spiritual victory over sin by the Holy Spirit, who indwells every true believer. As we turn over our lives to Him and allow Him to take control, He will deliver us from the power of indwelling sin by occupying us with Christ and changing us into Christ's likeness. The question, then, that Paul answers in this chapter is:

"How, then, can I live a holy life?"

A holy life is the result of the Holy Spirit having His way in the believer's life. The results of this are numerous and blessed.

Whereas efforts at law-keeping produce only bondage, life in Christ is perfect freedom.

First of all, there is *a new freedom* (v. 1). "There is therefore now no condemnation to those who are in Christ Jesus." Whereas efforts at law-keeping produce only bondage, life in Christ is perfect freedom.

Then there is *a new law of life* (v. 2). "The law of the Spirit of life in Christ Jesus" has superseded "the law of sin and death." This may be illustrated as follows: When you throw a stone into the air, it immediately returns to the earth. The law of gravity has taken effect. When you toss a living bird into the air, however, it flies off into the heavens. A new law has taken effect—one that is greater than the law of gravity. It is the law of life. Thus there is a principle in every Christian like the law of gravity, always seeking to drag him down into sin. But the indwelling Holy Spirit is able to free the believer from the law of sin and death.

There is *a new power* (vv. 3-4). The Law could not produce righteousness because of the fallen condition of human nature. But Christ, by His death, condemned sin in human nature, and ended its power over His people. Now the Christian is able to fulfill the righteousness of the Law by the power of the Holy Spirit.

There are *new desires* (v. 5). The Holy Spirit directs the believer's mind away from things that please the flesh and seeks to occupy him with the things in which God is interested.

Life and peace become the believer's experience. This is true life—life that is worth living.

There are *new results* (v. 6). Life and peace become the believer's experience. This is true life—life that is worth living. It is Christ's life, reproduced in us.

There is *a new attitude toward God* (v. 7). Loving submission replaces enmity and rebellion.

There is *a new sphere of life*—in the Spirit rather than in the flesh (vv. 8-9). A person living in the flesh caters to his own desires and comforts. He acts as if his body and his possessions were the only things that really count. A person living in the Spirit turns his life over to God so that the Holy Spirit may have His way without being hindered.

There is *a new guarantee* (v. 11). The Holy Spirit in the child of God is definite proof that his body will be raised from the dead, just as Christ's was.

There is *a new allegiance* (v. 12). We owe all our loyalty to the Spirit, not to the flesh. We owe nothing to the flesh.

There is *a new duty* (v. 13). We are to put to death (mortify) the deeds of the body through the power of the Holy Spirit. This means to say no to every thought or deed that is unworthy of the Lord Jesus.

There is *a new guidance* (v. 14). True Christians enjoy the enviable privilege of being led by the Spirit of God. Instead of aimless wandering, there is planned progress in life.

There is *a new sense of intimacy with God* (v. 15). It is the freedom of a son rather than the fear of a slave. We can look up into the face of God by faith and call Him "Father."

There are *new relationships* (vv. 16-17). The Spirit teaches the Christian that he is a *child* of God by birth (John 1:12-13) and a *son* of God by adoption—he will inherit special privileges as an heir of God and a joint-heir with Christ. Since we are members of God's family, it follows that we will share all the Father's riches with Christ.

There is *a new privilege* (vv. 17-18, 20-23). It is to suffer with Christ. This might not seem like much of a privilege at first. But when you realize that the Lord Jesus shares every pain, it becomes a blessing.

There is *a new hope* (vv. 23-24). It is the redemption of the body. God's work in us will not be complete until He has taken these frail bodies of ours and freed them forever from the power and presence of sin.

There is *a new prospect* (vv. 17-19). We are going to be glorified with Christ. The whole creation, including the animal kingdom, is waiting for the time when we will be displayed as the sons of God, the co-heirs of Christ (v. 19). At present, this is a groaning, sobbing world, but a better day is coming, and for that day we hope (*hope* being understood as "confident expectation" in this context).

There is *a new assistance* (vv. 26-27). We often find it hard to know how to pray because we do not know God's will in the matters that we are concerned about. The indwelling Spirit knows God's will and intercedes on our behalf, expressing those requests in line with God's will. The context implies prayer about spiritual issues.

There is *a new confidence* (vv. 28-30). God is on our side.

Finally, there is *a new assurance* (vv. 31-39). No one can be successfully against us. We are on the winning side. We are more than conquerors!

Verses 33 through 39 of this chapter have been much loved by Christians of all ages and in all countries. Those who take the time to memorize them will be well rewarded.

CHAPTER 8 EXAM

Use the exam sheet that has been provided to complete your exam

1. **The believer is delivered from the power of indwelling sin by**
   A. the indwelling Holy Spirit.
   B. putting on the whole armor of God.
   C. separating oneself from the world.

2. **Romans 8 begins with**
   A. there is no justification.
   B. there is no condemnation.
   C. there is no separation.

3. **The law of sin and death has been overcome by**
   A. the law of God which is holy and just.
   B. the law of the mind.
   C. the law of the Spirit of life in Christ Jesus.

4. **The Holy Spirit in the child of God guarantees that**
   A. he will never sin again.
   B. now his old nature is gone.
   C. one day his body will be raised as Christ's body was.

5. **What should the Christian do with the deeds of the body?**
   A. Boast about them
   B. Mortify them (put them to death)
   C. Multiply them for our pleasure

6. **What is NOT a teaching of Romans 8 for the believer?**
   A. Being guided by the Holy Spirit
   B. Being a joint-heir with Christ
   C. Being exempt from suffering

7. **Which stage is NOT yet completed in the believer?**
   A. The redemption of his spirit
   B. The redemption of his soul
   C. The redemption of his body

8. **All creation is waiting for the day when**
   A. believers will be displayed as the children of God.
   B. man will rule over all the forces of nature.
   C. the end of the world will come.

9. **The Holy Spirit makes intercession for the saints**
   A. that match our own.
   B. according to the will of God.
   C. to make our prayers valid.

10. **God assures believers in Christ that**
    A. they will never suffer harm.
    B. no one can successfully stand against them.
    C. they will be healthy and wealthy.

What Do You Say?

What theme in Romans 8 has been the greatest blessing to you?

____

____

____

____

LESSON 9

The Case of the Jew

Romans 9:1–11:36

During the Old Testament period, God's dealings were primarily with the nation of Israel. They were His chosen people, and it was to them that He made many great and precious promises.

Now that the gospel message was being preached to Gentiles as well as Jews, it almost seemed as if God had forgotten about these ancient promises. So the next question in an enquirer's mind was:

"Has God broken His promises to the Jews?"

No! Paul here explains that Israel has been temporarily set aside by God because of its unbelief. However, when the nation again turns to the Lord, it will be restored to a position of privilege and favor.

We will consider the subject under three main headings.

1. Israel's Rejection Was Justified (9:1-29)

The nation had been highly favored. God had chosen them to be His own people; they had the glory cloud, which signified His presence on earth; they had the covenants, the law of Moses, the temple service, the promises, and the patriarchs. Finally, the Lord Jesus was descended from Israel. In spite of all this, Israel rejected the Messiah and so has been set aside by God (vv. 1-5).

This does not mean, however, that God had been unfaithful to His promise. His promises were never made to *all* Israel, but always to a chosen, or elect, portion (v. 6). For instance, Abraham had many children, but only the descendants of Isaac were the ones God chose to be the means of blessing—the channel through which the Messiah would come—to the world. The mere fact of one's ancestry does not insure blessing; Rebecca had twin sons, Jacob and Esau; but the line of promise was only through Jacob. God made this clear before the boys were born, thus indicating that good works had nothing to do with His decision.

It will be seen, then, that God is sovereign. He will show mercy to whomever He pleases (vv. 14-18). No one can accuse Him of unfairness (v. 14). He told Moses that He would do this (v. 15). It is not a matter of man's effort, but of God's mercy (v. 16). When Pharaoh hardened his heart against God, God used him as an object lesson by which to demonstrate His power (v. 17).

No one has a right to question God's actions (vv. 19-21). To do so puts man on an even footing with God. All human beings come from the same lump of sinful clay. If left alone, we would all perish. God is the Potter. As such, He comes into His "workshop" and shows mercy to some. Does He not have the right to do this? As Charles Erdman says, "God's sovereignty is never exercised in condemning men who ought to be saved, but rather it has resulted in the salvation of men who ought to be lost."

God only rejected Israel after much patient long-suffering (vv. 22-24). What's more, the salvation of Gentiles and the rejection of all but a remnant of Israel was predicted in the Old Testament. The salvation of Gentiles is discussed in verses 25 and 26, and the rejection of all but a remnant of Israel is discussed in verses 27-29.

2. Israel's Rejection Is Due to Unbelief (9:30–10:21)

The Jews sought to obtain righteousness in their own way—that is, by trying to keep the Law (9:30-33). In other words, they refused to submit to God's way of salvation, which is by exercising faith in Christ (10:1-4). Israel should have known from the Old Testament that righteousness is by faith, not by law (10:5-11) because Moses taught the difference. Law tells man to *do,* but faith says there is *nothing to do,* because Christ has already *done* the work. He came down into the world, He died, He was buried, and He rose again. What God required of the Jews (and of all people) is to confess Jesus as Lord and believe that God raised Him from the dead. The Jews, as a people, denied both the deity of Jesus and His bodily resurrection, so Paul focused on these key essential doctrines as tests of belief.

Israel should also have known from the Old Testament that righteousness by faith is for all, both Jews and Gentiles (10:12-21). Many of the prophets foretold it. Isaiah proclaimed salvation for "whoever believes" (v. 11). Joel promised salvation for "whoever" also (v. 13). Isaiah and David both spoke of the world-wide proclamation of the gospel (vv. 15, 18). Moses and Isaiah both predicted the calling of the Gentiles (vv. 19-20), while Isaiah foresaw the rejection of the message by Israel (v. 21).

3. Israel's Rejection Is Neither Complete Nor Final (11:1-36)

God did not reject the entire nation (vv. 1-6). The apostle himself was proof of this (v. 1). Also, a remnant has been preserved by grace, even as in the days of Elijah (vv. 2-5). However, God caused blindness to come upon Israel (vv. 7-10)—not physical blindness, of course, but an inability to see clearly in spiritual matters. Note also that Israel's rejection does not mean the nation will be cut off forever (vv. 11-16). Their rejection has resulted in salvation coming to the Gentiles (vv. 11-12). Moreover, Gentile blessing was intended to provoke the Jewish nation to jealousy (v. 14).

If Israel's downfall has meant blessing to the world, its restoration will mean even greater blessing (vv. 15-16). Gentiles, however, should beware of the same peril which caused Israel's rejection (vv. 17-25). They should not boast. The Jews, after all, are the channel of blessing. They were rejected because of their unbelief. In verses 17-24, Paul uses the figure of an olive tree to illustrate his teaching. The natural olive branches are the nation of Israel. The wild olive branches are the Gentiles. The olive tree itself illustrates *the line of privilege* throughout the history of the world. Unbelief, therefore, is just as much a peril to the Gentiles as it was to the Jews (vv. 21-22). It would be a much less disruptive process for God to restore Israel than it was to bring the Gentile people into blessing (vv. 22-24). Israel's blindness is only temporary (v. 25), for the nation will yet be restored (vv. 26-32).

Israel's rejection has resulted in salvation coming to the Gentiles.

Paul's conclusion is that God's ways are wonderfully perfect (vv. 33-36). The student should pay special attention to these verses. They really teach the truth that God is everything, and man is nothing.

CHAPTER 9 EXAM

Use the exam sheet that has been provided to complete your exam

1. **Paul discusses "the Jewish question" because**
   A. they were excluded from the offer of salvation.
   B. they were exempt from the offer of salvation.
   C. Israel has been temporarily set aside by God.

2. **What is NOT included in the list of Israel's blessings?**
   A. The adoption
   B. The cloud as a sign of God's presence
   C. Victory over all their foes in Canaan

3. **The promises of God in Old Testament times were**
   A. conditional, if Israel would accept the Messiah.
   B. made only to the nation as a whole, not to individuals.
   C. given only to an elect group within the nation of Israel.

4. **God's choice of Jacob over Esau proved that His blessing**
   A. depends on a person's good works.
   B. is dependent on God's sovereign purpose.
   C. depends on a person keeping religious rites.

5. **Pharaoh's position illustrates God's sovereignty in**
   A. His Person and triune Godhead.
   B. His mercy and His judgment.
   C. His creation of the world.

6. **Which of the following best describes divine election?**
   A. God elects some people to be saved and some to be damned
   B. God elects all to be damned but some to be saved
   C. God saves some who ought to be lost

7. **The setting aside of Israel is attributed by Paul to the**
   A. original purpose of God made clear in the promises.
   B. nation's refusal of salvation through Jesus Christ.
   C. Gentiles being more worthy of blessings than the Jews.

8. **God requires both Jews and Gentiles ___________ in order to attain righteousness.**
   A. to obey the 10 commandments and love their neighbors
   B. to worship God regularly and do good works
   C. to confess Jesus as Lord and believe God raised Him from the dead

9. **The setting aside of Israel is**
   A. a permanent thing.
   B. a temporary thing.
   C. dependent on what the Gentiles do with the gospel.

10. **What does the symbol of the olive tree represent?**
   A. Privileged people through the world's history
   B. The privileged Jewish nation in Old Testament times
   C. The church inheriting the spiritual blessings of the Jews

What Do You Say?

Where have you seen evidence of God's sovereignty in your life?

____

____

____

____

LESSON 10

Love Fulfills the Law

Romans 12:1–13:14

We now come to what is known as the practical part of the letter. The earlier chapters have revealed what God has done for us. Now we learn how we should respond to Him by lives of devotion and service.

"How should Christians behave?"

There are a number of obligations which rest on those who have been saved by grace.

Our lives should be yielded to Him moment by moment so He can use us in whatever way He pleases.

Consecration to God is the first of these obligations (vv. 1-2). These verses are certainly among the most important in the letter, and it would be a tragedy to finish the course and yet miss their message. As Paul considers all that God has done (as revealed in the previous chapters), he feels impelled to make a very strong appeal to his readers: "Present your bodies a living sacrifice, holy, acceptable to God."

The mercies of God to the sinner saved by grace leave him with only one reasonable conclusion: "If God has done all this for me, then I must give my body to Him. If Christ died for me, the least I can do is to live for Him."

In the words of the hymn by Isaac Watts, *When I Survey the Wondrous Cross*:

> Were the whole realm of nature mine,
> That were an offering far too small;

Love so amazing, so divine,
Demands my heart, my life, my all.

These words are true. In fact, one of the greatest contradictions in the universe is a Christian who lives to please himself rather than the Lord who bought him. Our lives should be yielded to Him moment by moment so He can use us in whatever way He pleases.

Paul now urges his readers not to be conformed to the world. We should be different. Instead of thinking like the world does, we should look at things as God sees them. After all, it was the world that crucified our Savior, and so we should be separated from it in all our thoughts and ways.

As we thus yield our bodies to God, and renew our minds by thinking His thoughts, we will come to know what His good, acceptable, and perfect will is for us, and then our lives will really count for eternity.

Humility in the exercise of gifts is another obligation (vv. 3-8). Everything we have has been given to us from above. We should not be proud, therefore, of any special abilities we may have, but should simply seek to use them for His glory.

Sacrificial love to the saints is commanded of believers (vv. 9-13). Our love should be sincere, pure, unselfish, and kind.

We should demonstrate love to our persecutors as well (vv. 14-21). The Christian should not seek revenge, but leave the matter of judgment to God. The best policy is to repay persecution with kindness.

Christians are expected to subject themselves to the government currently in power (13:1-7). Since it is God who ordains the civil powers, the child of God should be obedient, not just out of fear of punishment, but for the sake of conscience. Of course, the Christian's first loyalty is to God, and he should not let any government compel him to go against anything commanded in God's written Word. However, in matters of paying taxes and customs, the believer has definite obligations to the higher powers.

Love to the lost is a Christian obligation (vv. 8-10) a debt we owe to all people.

Let me look on the crowd as my Savior did,
Till my eyes with tears grow dim.
Let me view with pity the wandering sheep,
And love them for love of Him.

Watchful waiting for the Lord's return characterizes the believer (vv. 11-14). Everything we do should be judged by the fact that the time is short, as Christ will soon come to take us home to be with Him. The twofold secret of Christian living is (1) to put on the Lord Jesus Christ, that is, be so occupied with Him and so anxious to please Him that others will see Him in us; and (2) to make no provision for the flesh by walking in the Spirit. We must refuse the promptings and passions of the flesh. We must not cater to it or take its influence lightly, but instead "by the Spirit [...] put to death the deeds of the body" (8:13).

CHAPTER 10 EXAM

Use the exam sheet that has been provided to complete your exam

1. **Believers should present their bodies to God based on**
   A. the mercies of God.
   B. the sacrifices demanded by the law.
   C. Paul's personal experience.

2. **The rest of Romans tells us how we should respond to God**
   A. because of His tendency to wrath.
   B. because of what He has done for us.
   C. because of the uncertainty of our salvation.

3. **The plea that the Christian present his body to God is**
   A. to be understood in a mystical sense only.
   B. is very unreasonable.
   C. declared to be his reasonable service.

4. **The believer's response to the world should be**
   A. to become like it.
   B. to refuse to be squeezed into its mold.
   C. to antagonize it deliberately.

5. **A Christian convinced of a call to missions should**
   A. wait until everyone agrees with him.
   B. count the cost and go knowing it is God's will.
   C. send someone in his place and support him.

6. **A believer who is obviously greatly gifted and capable should**
   A. use his gifts for his own benefit.
   B. humbly use them for others.
   C. have a very high opinion of himself.

7. **We should love other Christians**
   - A. sacrificially.
   - B. conditionally.
   - C. selfishly.

8. **The Christian's attitude towards one who persecutes him should be**
   - A. to ignore him.
   - B. to pay him back.
   - C. to show him kindness.

9. **If the demands of the government do not contradict God's rules, Christians**
   - A. must try to change the government.
   - B. must obey only what they think is reasonable.
   - C. must obey the government.

10. **A Christian faced with disobedience to the Word of God because of the government should**
    - A. obey the government because it is ordained of God.
    - B. protest, but obey the law.
    - C. be loyal to God and the Bible.

What Do You Say?

Explain why you chose the answer you did for question 10.

____

____

____

____

LESSON 11

The Weak and the Strong

Romans 14:1–15:13

Paul has been showing how a Christian should conduct himself in various relationships both within and outside the sphere of Christian fellowship. Now He deals with a most practical issue indeed:

"How should Christians treat one another?"

Tolerance to the brother who is weak is an important rule of Christian conduct. The apostle here begins a discussion of two types of Christians, the weak and the strong. In this first-century context, the "weak" brother was one who felt he could not, as a believer now, eat certain types of food, or who felt bound to observe certain religious days. Perhaps this type of person was originally of Jewish background and continued to hold some of these beliefs after his conversion.

The "strong" brother is one who realizes that these matters are not important to God. The Christian (again, using the issues current in those days) was free to eat all kinds of wholesome foods, and was under no obligation to observe certain days of the year in a special way.

Realizing that the presence of these two types of individuals might cause conflict in the church, Paul now urges a spirit of loving tolerance to one another. First, he addresses them individually, then unitedly. (It should be noted that the principles set down here only apply to inconsequential matters, such as food and drink. They must not be applied to doctrines or duties which are clearly taught in the Bible. Think carefully about the kinds of issues that this principle relates to today.)

To the strong, Paul's instruction is: Receive the weak brother into your fellowship, and not with the goal of starting a controversy with him (v. 1). You should not despise the weak brother (v. 3a). To the weak he says, Do not condemn the strong brother (v. 3b); after all, God has received him (v. 3b). He is God's servant and accountable to God (v. 4). You may think he will fall into sin because of his attitude, but God will keep him from falling (v. 4).

Paul now appeals to both the strong and the weak: Let every individual be fully persuaded in his own mind about these matters of moral indifference. Christ is our Lord, and we must do all with a view to pleasing Him (vv. 5-9). Let us not judge others. We will have to give an account of *ourselves*, not others, at the judgment seat of Christ (vv. 10-13a). Let us not be a cause of offense to others (vv. 13b-15). Things that are harmless to some are sinful to others. We are wrong if we grieve others over such matters. It does not show true love for them. To tempt them to sin is to wreck those for whom Christ died; they might become discouraged and cease to make progress in the Christian life, for instance. Let not your good be evil spoken of (vv. 16-18). The things that really count are not material, such as food and drink, but spiritual. Those who recognize this distinction are approved by God. Let us adopt this twofold standard—does it make for peace, and does it edify, or build up (vv. 19-23)?

We will have to give an account of ourselves at the judgment seat of Christ.

If we follow this rule, we will not let inconsequential things wreck the work God is doing in another believer's life. We will do nothing that would cause a brother to stumble, or be offended, or be made weak. We will not proudly parade our Christian liberty. We will not do what our conscience condemns.

Let us live to please others more than ourselves (15:2-6). The Savior did not please Himself; certainly, we should follow His example. Therefore, let us receive one another (15:7-13). Christ has received both Jew and Gentile, so we should receive both weak and strong.

CHAPTER 11 EXAM

Use the exam sheet that has been provided to complete your exam

1. **In Paul's day, the "weak brother"**
   A. felt he should not eat certain types of food.
   B. observed certain days for religious purposes.
   C. was characterized by both of the above.

2. **The "strong brother" is the Christian who**
   A. abstains from certain types of food and drink
   B. always attends every meeting at church
   C. realizes special diets and days have no bearing on vital Christianity

3. **The principles shown in this section of Romans apply**
   A. only to relatively inconsequential issues.
   B. to major doctrines.
   C. to Christian duty and doctrine.

4. **One who feels Easter and Christmas must be strictly observed**
   A. should be refused acceptance in the local church.
   B. should be accepted and everyone agree with him.
   C. should be received into fellowship and not condemned

5. **Both weak and strong brothers ____________ about matters of moral indifference.**
   A. should follow the conscience of the other
   B. should be fully persuaded in his own mind
   C. should ignore the conscience of the other

6. **A person's actions are to be determined by his relationship to**
   A. circumstances.
   B. the Lord.
   C. the faith.

7. **Which admonition is NOT found in Romans 14?**
   A. Let every man be fully persuaded in his own mind.
   B. Let us not be weary in well doing.
   C. Let us not be a cause of offense to others.

8. **In view of the judgment seat of Christ, it would be good to**
   A. tell all "weak" brethren we know to "grow up."
   B. tell all "strong" brethren to give up their rights.
   C. take heed to one's own life.

9. **The rule of life for the believer should be**
   A. to always do what is right in his own eyes.
   B. to let his conscience be his guide.
   C. to be sure his behavior makes for peace and edification.

10. **We should receive both strong and weak into our fellowship because**
   A. Christ has received them.
   B. it will make for a peaceful relationship.
   C. it is the tolerant thing to do.

What Do You Say?

What is your attitude towards those who differ from you about "non-essential" issues?

____

____

____

____

LESSON 12

People and Places

Romans 15:14–16:27

The time has come for Paul to conclude his letter. He has discussed the need for the gospel, its nature, and its implications. He concludes with a brief discussion of his plans and some personal greetings.

Paul's Plans

First of all, Paul gives his reasons for writing the letter (vv. 14-21). He wanted to remind them of these great truths so that his work as the Apostle to the Gentiles might be acceptable to God.

Next, Paul discusses his plans for the immediate future (vv. 22-33). He hopes to visit Rome on his trip to Spain. In the meantime, however, he is going to Jerusalem with a gift of money for the needy saints there from the Christians in Macedonia and Achaia. In view of his plans, he asks them to pray for the success of his mission in Jerusalem, for deliverance from unbelievers, and for blessing on his ministry when he reaches Rome.

How fitting to close this letter with a picture of truth in action!

Personal Greetings

At first glance, the closing chapter of Romans seems to be an uninteresting catalog of names that have little or no meaning to us today. However, on closer study, this neglected chapter yields many precious lessons for the believer.

The Christians listed here are living examples of the truths taught in the letter. How fitting it is to close this letter with a picture of truth in action! Paul shows a deep personal interest in, and love for, the saints. He was pleased to hear of their progress and delighted with their steadfast devotion to Christ. We should maintain the same attitude toward our fellow-believers.

Some Bible students have made the interesting suggestion that Romans 16 is a miniature of the judgment seat of Christ. There is praise for every instance of faithfulness to the Lord here. The entire chapter is a commentary on Christian greatness. These people were not famous as far as the world was concerned, but their names are recorded forever in God's written Word.

> **God rewards every kindness done in His name.**

Personal names often have meanings which are interesting and instructive. For instance, Epaenetus means "praiseworthy," and Philologus means "lover of the word." No doubt, these men lived up to their names.

Letter writing is a great ministry. We never know how God will use what we write when we write for His glory and to help and encourage His people. God rewards every kindness done in His name. This section shows that little deeds of kindness are noticed and recorded by Him.

The chapter shows that letters of commendation were carried by Christians going from one church, or assembly, to another (v. 1). This is a means of excluding unbelievers and imposters from the fellowship of the local church. The prominence of women's names in this chapter emphasizes their widespread involvement in the work of the church (vv. 1, 3, 6, 7, etc.).

> **Hospitality is mentioned often and commended always.**

This closing section is an outstanding example of Christian community. The chapter evidences a lack of officialism and class distinctions among the saints. They were "all one in Christ Jesus." It is clear that a very close fellowship existed among the believers. Their Christian faith seems to have been the absorbing passion of their lives, and this common interest bound them together. The simplicity of the New Testament church is suggested. As we read in verse 5, "the church that is in their house," we can picture a group of believers meeting in a home for worship, prayer, teaching, and fellowship.

In verses 17-19 we have a warning against those who cause divisions. It is a warning, incidentally, that is still needed today.

Finally, we learn that hospitality must be very important in God's estimation, because it is mentioned often and commended always.

And now at the conclusion of our study of this wonderful letter, we would say along with Paul, "The grace of our Lord Jesus Christ be with you all! Amen."

CHAPTER 12 EXAM

Use the exam sheet that has been provided to complete your exam

1. **What place did Paul plan to visit on his way to Spain?**
   A. Crete
   B. Macedonia
   C. Rome

2. **Paul was planning to visit Jerusalem to**
   A. discuss his plans with the other apostles.
   B. gain financial support for churches in Europe.
   C. deliver a gift from the Gentile churches.

3. **The people mentioned by Paul in his closing chapter**
   A. needed to be rebuked for being bad examples.
   B. were living examples of the truth taught in Romans.
   C. were all his converts in Rome.

4. **The author of the course observes that Romans 16 resembles a miniature of the scene at the**
   A. judgment seat of Christ.
   B. great white throne judgment.
   C. gates of heaven.

5. **What did Paul especially note about the Roman believers?**
   A. Their great and spectacular achievements
   B. The little things they had done
   C. Their generosity in giving financially

6. **One reason for letters of commendations from one church to another was to**
   A. praise the one carrying the letter.
   B. eliminate imposters from fellowship in the local church.
   C. ask for money from the receiving church.

7. **Chapter 16 indicates**
   A. there was an official hierarchy in the church.
   B. there was a lack of class distinction among the saints.
   C. there was much discord in the church at Rome.

8. **Where were the Christians in Rome meeting at this time?**
   A. With great simplicity, in private homes
   B. In ornate church buildings
   C. In the catacombs because of persecution

9. **Verses 17-19 contain a warning against those who**
   A. teach false doctrine.
   B. leave the church.
   C. cause divisions in the church.

10. **Paul's final word in Romans repeats**
    A. the letter's great theme—the grace of the Lord Jesus Christ.
    B. his promise to visit Rome in the will of the Lord.
    C. the truth of the Lord's second coming.

What Do You Say?

What has this study of Romans meant to you?

And do not be conformed to this world, but be transformed by the renewing of your mind, that you may prove what is that good and acceptable and perfect will of God. For I say, through the grace given to me, to everyone who is among you, not to think of himself more highly than he ought to think, but to think soberly, as God has dealt to each one a measure of faith.

—Romans 12:2-3